We Need Insects!

By Anna Prokos

CELEBRATION PRESS
Pearson Learning Group

W9-AAO-947

Contents

Introduction

Don't squash that bug! Each day many insects help us and our planet. Without insects, Earth would be a very different place.

European wasp

bumble bees

The Earth Needs Insects

Insects are an important part of nature.
Some insects help plants grow. Some eat other
harmful insects. Some insects keep the soil healthy.
Many insects are food for other living things.
Some even make things we use. We need insects.

▲ These ants are moving
the body of a grasshopper.

◀ **Chalkhill blue
butterfly**

Some insects can be **pests**. These insects are harmful to people, plants, and other animals. Some pests, such as mosquitoes, bite humans and animals. Other pests damage plants. Often though these insects are also food for helpful insects and other animals. So sometimes we need pests, too.

Large groups of **aphids** can damage a plant.

brown aphid

green aphid

Insects Help Plants Grow

We need insects to help plants grow. Bees, wasps, flies, moths, and butterflies all fly from flower to flower to sip nectar, a sweet liquid. When they land on a flower, pollen sticks to their bodies. Pollen is a powder on flowers.

bumble bee   **pollen**

When insects fly from flower to flower, they spread the pollen. Plants need pollen to make seeds. The seeds then grow into new plants. So the pollen spread by insects helps new fruits, vegetables, and flowers grow every day. The next time you eat a fruit or vegetable, thank an insect!

pumpkin

watermelon

pear

broccoli

carrots

Insects spread the pollen that helps fruits and vegetables grow.

Good Insects, Good Eaters

Insects that are helpful to humans are called **beneficial insects.** Many beneficial insects are **predators**. They eat pests. Ladybugs are great predators. Some ladybugs can eat more than 50 aphids a day. That's good for a farmer because a group of tiny aphids can damage a whole plant.

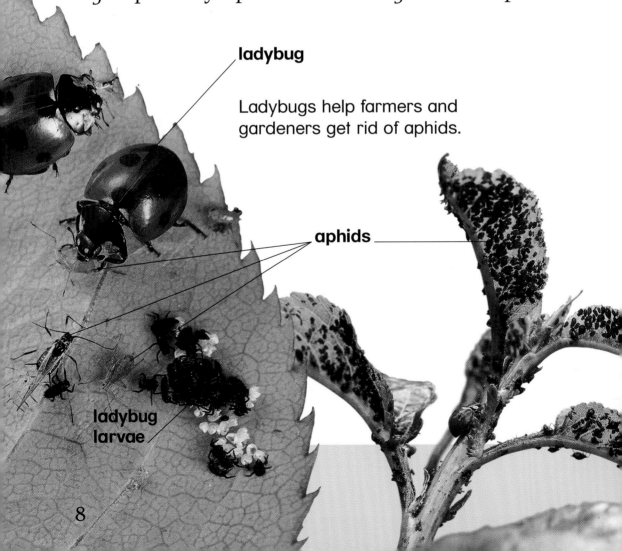

ladybug

Ladybugs help farmers and gardeners get rid of aphids.

aphids

ladybug larvae

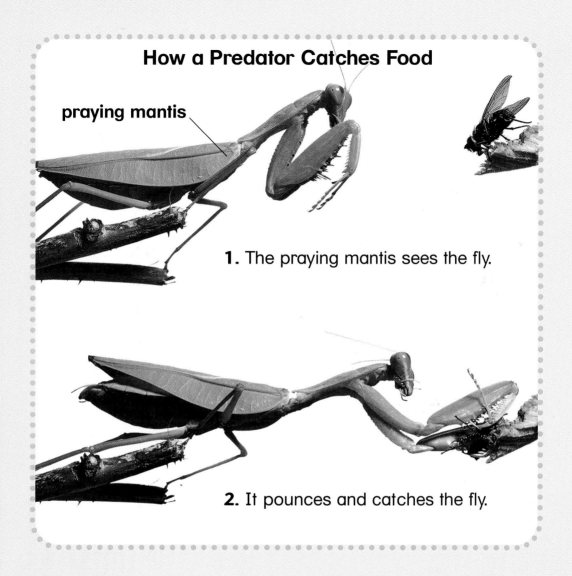

How a Predator Catches Food

praying mantis

1. The praying mantis sees the fly.

2. It pounces and catches the fly.

Farmers like to have certain predator insects in their fields. That way they don't have to use as many chemicals to kill pests. These chemicals can be harmful to people and animals.

Some beneficial insects are **parasites**. Many parasites lay eggs on or in pest insects. The eggs hatch into **larvae**, or young insects. As the larvae grow, they eat the pest insect.

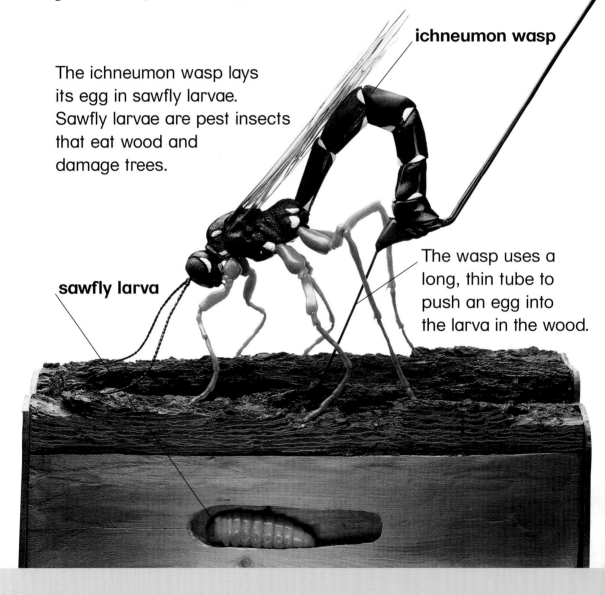

ichneumon wasp

The ichneumon wasp lays its egg in sawfly larvae. Sawfly larvae are pest insects that eat wood and damage trees.

sawfly larva

The wasp uses a long, thin tube to push an egg into the larva in the wood.

10

Marigolds were planted in this garden to attract hover flies.
The hover fly larvae will eat pest insects in the garden.

Smart gardeners find ways to bring beneficial
insect predators to their gardens. They attract
the insects by growing certain plants. The insects
like certain plants and flowers.

Some beneficial insects have big appetites! Lacewing larvae can eat hundreds of aphids in a day. They also like caterpillars and insect eggs. A hover fly larva can eat 50 aphids a day, or up to 400 in its lifetime! An insect called the assassin bug is a hunter. These bugs feed on many different insects.

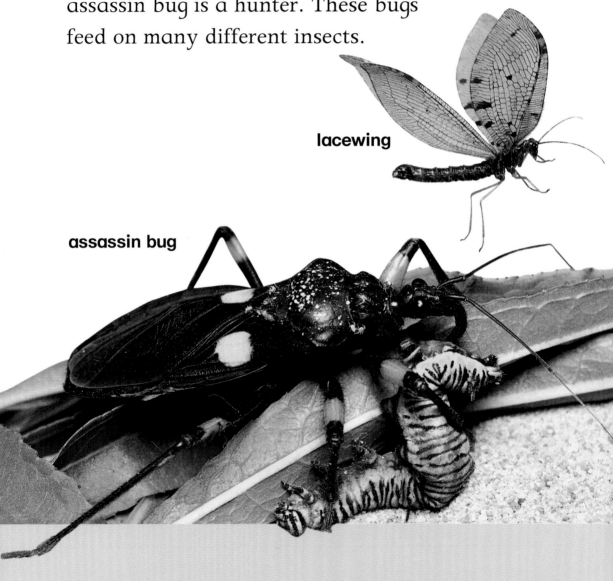

lacewing

assassin bug

Insects Help the Soil

Imagine stepping on dead plants and animals on your walk to school. That's what might happen if insects weren't around. **Maggots**, or fly larvae, and some grown insects are **decomposers**. They get rid of unhealthy things in the environment.

This beetle is feeding on a bat skeleton.

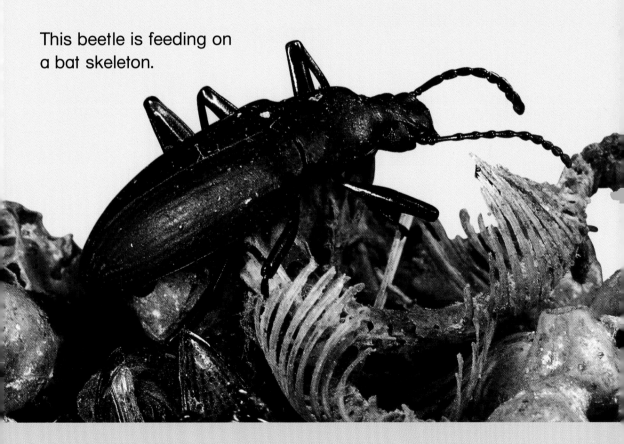

Decomposers eat dead plants and animals and animal waste. That puts nutrients back into the soil. By doing this, they help make the soil richer.

◀ a group of dung beetles feeding

A dung beetle is a decomposer. It feeds on animal waste. ▶

Insects Are Food

Insects are part of a day's meal for many animals. Some birds eat hundreds of insects in one day. Bats and frogs eat insects, too. These animals need insects to survive.

The frog catches a fly with its sticky tongue.

Animals aren't the only ones who eat insects. People do, too. In many places people feast on all kinds of insects. Many of these insects are good for you.

▲ This tortilla with roasted grasshoppers and avocado is from a restaurant in Mexico.

◀ This man in Uganda is eating white flying ants.

In Thailand a woman cooks locusts. ▶

Insects Provide Things We Use

Insects help make all sorts of things that people use. If it weren't for bees, we wouldn't have honey to eat. If it weren't for silkworms, we wouldn't have silk. The table below lists some of the things insects provide.

Products That Come From Insects

Insect	Products
bee	honey beeswax
silkworm (larva of silk moth)	silk
cochineal insects	red dye

Bees Produce Honey

These white cells contain honey.

Bees give us honey. Beeswax from bee hives can be made into candles.

Silkworms Produce Silk

The silkworm makes a cocoon of silk.

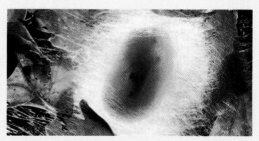

The silk protects the silkworm while it grows.

Insects Are Beautiful

Many people think insects are beautiful. Some people collect them. The different colors, shapes, and sizes of insects are amazing. Many zoos have gardens where people can see the beauty of insects.

garden chafer beetle

stripe-winged grasshopper

cardinal beetle

mullein moth
caterpillar

seven-spot ladybug

21

We Need Insects!

What would life be like without insects? Some plants might not produce as many fruits and vegetables. Many plants might be damaged or destroyed. Dead plants and animals might stay on the ground longer. Some animals might need to find other food. People wouldn't have many things we use every day. So the next time you raise your foot to stomp on an insect, walk around it instead.

Glossary

aphids
tiny insects that feed by sucking sap from plants

beneficial insects
kinds of insects that destroy pests

decomposers
animals that eat dead plants and animals and animal waste

larvae
young insects that look like worms and caterpillars; singular *larva*

maggots
the larvae of a fly

parasites
animals that live in or on another living thing

pests
animals that harm people, plants, or other animals

predators
animals that kill or eat other animals for food

Index